PRAISE *for* LIM-ERIC!

"Having broadcast Cardinal games for over a decade, this book makes me realize I did not use the countless hours in the booth to my advantage. Hall of Famer Eric Nadel will make you laugh and think with his limericks. The illustrations are gorgeous and remind me of the fun and beauty of our national pastime. This is a must for any baseball fan!"

-- JOE BUCK,
FOX-TV

"A scintillating journey through the inner workings of the enigma known as Eric Nadel -- master of all trades, jack of none. Honestly, I thought it was going to be about tennis."

-- GARTH STEIN,
New York Times bestselling author of a book narrated by a dog, and by no means an authority on limericks.

"Some people say the world doesn't need a book of limericks penned by a brilliant Hall Of Fame broadcaster. Those people are jerks."

-- RHETT MILLER,
Lead Singer, Old 97's

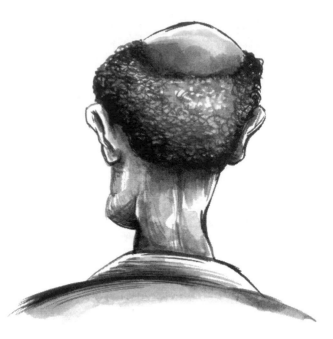

"I'm more of a sonnet man myself, but these are very good!!"

-- RON WASHINGTON,
Atlanta Braves 3B coach, Former Texas Rangers Manager

"Eric Nadel is one of the best and smartest play-by-play guys ever. His new book is so clever, so funny, so beautifully written and illustrated. I loved it!"

-- TIM KURKJIAN,
ESPN and ESPN The Magazine

"As neither a math, English, literature, science, or arts aficionado, I have no clear picture how these writing concepts should play out... but Eric Nadel is the writer, so it is awesome."

-- MICHAEL YOUNG,
Seven-time All-Star, Texas Rangers Hall of Fame

"Eric Nadel has already secured his place among the greatest "Voices of the Game" in the Baseball Hall of Fame. Now, he rubs elbows with Shakespeare (yes, the Bard dabbled in limerickery in at least 3 plays!) in his cool book of baseball limericks. Eric 'The Bard' Nadel!"

-- JON MILLER,
Voice of the SF Giants

"This is one of the funniest poetry books ever written about a last-place team. I can't wait for 2019 when Eric combines his three big loves - baseball, music and rhymes - to record his first rap album."

-- EVAN GRANT,
Dallas Morning News

"A witty book and a cry for help."

-- KEN LEVINE,
Emmy-winning Writer of Mash,
Cheers and Frasier

"I've known Eric Nadel for over 30 years and have always enjoyed him as an entertaining baseball broadcaster. This book of limericks shows he is a very creative writer, as well."

-- NOLAN RYAN,
Hall of Fame Pitcher,
All-time Strikeout King

By ERIC NADEL

*Whimsical Rhymes From
the Voice of the Texas Rangers and his Friends*

ILLUSTRATION *By* ARTHUR JAMES

PRINCIPITO PUBLISHING

Dallas • Pawtucket • Saskatoon • Sancti Spiritu

Cover Design / Illustrations by Arthur James
Text Design by Santiago Botello
Edited by Allyson Aynesworth

Grateful acknowledgement is made to those granting us permission to use their names or likenesses or to print the limericks they submitted.

The Texas Rangers Baseball Foundation is dedicated to improving the lives of children in need within our community by providing funding for youth in crisis, health initiatives, baseball programs, and education. For more information, www.texasrangers.com/foundation.

DEDICATION

*This book is dedicated to our loyal listeners
and my wonderful wife Jeannie...
for your kindness and sense of humor.*

TABLE *of* CONTENTS

INTRODUCTION

So how did all this limerick craziness get started? Actually… quite unexpectedly. The Rangers were playing the Red Sox at home on May 5th, and I was reading one of the live commercials that the team's marketing department gives us each game. This one was for a promotion they call "Pay the Day," where you could buy a ticket for $7 on May 7, and for $8 on May 8, for games against the Detroit Tigers.

At the end of the commercial was a silly little rhyme, "…you can pay the day because we're playing in May." After reading the commercial, I said to my broadcast partner Matt Hicks, "You know, if they are going to give us rhymes, why don't they at least write us a limerick?" To which he replied, "Well, why don't you?"

I accepted the challenge, took the copy home that night and wrote the following gems to use on the air the next day:

> **The Tigers are coming from Motown**
>
> **On Monday this week for a showdown.**
>
> **You can all pay the day,**
>
> **Since we're playing in May,**
>
> **But keep listening to us for the lowdown.**

AND…

The Tigers are bringing their team.

The excitement should be quite extreme.

You pay 7 or 8,

It is going to be great.

Come on out and get ready to scream!

That day, the Rangers were in the process of losing to the Red Sox, 6-1, dropping their record for the young season to 11-23. This called for what my former broadcast partner Mark Holtz used to term "diversionary tactics" to try to hold our audience. So, when Matt mentioned late in the game that a Red Sox prospect had just come up from their farm club, Pawtucket, I said, knowing full well the danger in rhyming with Pawtucket, "Hey, that sounds like the start of a limerick." Matt said, "OK, the guy from Pawtucket stepped into the bucket..." (a baseball phrase describing a batter who steps out to the side in his stride rather than toward the pitcher) "...you finish it!"

And thus, the "8th Inning Limerick of the Day" was born.

A young hitting star at Pawtucket,

Each time up would step into the bucket.

If he got this corrected,

He'd soon be selected

For Cooperstown, like Kirby Puckett.

This was just what we needed to amuse ourselves, and hopefully our audience, in a season that was shaping up as a long one. So I resolved to write a limerick each day and read it on the air in the 8th inning. Then I would post the limerick on Instagram and Twitter.

Sometimes Matt would write one, and occasionally our partner Jared Sandler would. And we would soon invite our listeners and friends to join in the fun, as well. Many of those are included in the chapter entitled "Pinch Hitters."

I've loved limericks since the 8th grade when my English teacher, Mrs. Rose, introduced us to the works of Edward Lear and Ogden Nash. I'll never forget, "There once was a lady from Niger, who smiled as she rode on a tiger…" And I had a knack for writing them almost immediately. When I was broadcasting minor league hockey, at times I would write limericks to pass the time with my co-workers.

The idea to put all the limericks in a book was suggested to me by many people, and the idea was crystalized when I was introduced to the amazing Arthur James, whose illustrations make these silly little rhymes come to life. Once I saw what he could do, I was determined to get the book done. It includes many limericks that were not used on the air, as I was restricted to using one per broadcast. And many of them are about subjects other than baseball.

A million thanks to the many people who helped make this book a reality… specifically our Project Manager Maureen Womack, who made sure that two spacey creative minds somehow met the deadlines to get the book published, Allyson Aynesworth, for providing ideas, editing and general wisdom, Carl Butzer, for invaluable legal advice, and John Blake and Karin Morris, whose wonderful Texas Rangers Baseball Foundation will receive a portion of the proceeds.

The real stars of this book are Arthur James, whose illustrations are beyond fantastic, and Santiago ("Bo") Botello, who designed most of the two-page spreads. Thanks, guys, for playing our game!

I owe a debt of thanks to my wife Jeannie for indulging this sometimes-irritating limerick habit… and of course, to those of you who pinch hit for me with limericks of your own.

And now… it's time for rhyme!

BASEBALL

DODGERS CODGERS

Going to Dodger Stadium brings back memories of the team leaving my hometown, Brooklyn, for LA when I was six years old.

My childhood team was the Dodgers,

With Snider and Koufax and Hodges.

They came out to LA

With intentions to stay,

And that still bugs us Brooklyn old codgers.

MY FAVORITE RANGER

My favorite Ranger is Beltre.
He has the charisma of Elway.
Just don't touch his head
Or you're going to be dead.
Don't want him to quit, fans? Well... then pray!

He has over 3,000 hits,
With shots too hard for fielders' mitts.
Throw him nasty low cheese,
He'll hit bombs from his knees.
He's given all those pitchers fits.

His dazzling plays come every game.
They're breathtaking, never the same.
With each Gold Glove miracle
The proof is empirical,
He's headed for the Hall of Fame.

He does all of this with a smile,
The playfulness of a small child.
Undeniable joy,
As if he's still a boy,
The man has unparalleled style.

"Cool at the hot corner"

HYPHENATED-BATTERY

The Rangers used the first all-hyphenated battery in MLB history on June 20 at KC, when Austin Bibens-Dirkx pitched and Isiah Kiner-Falefa caught.

It's IKF and Bibens-Dirkx.
We'll see if this battery works.
They both have shown flashes
And both names have dashes.
That's one of their lovable quirks.

YO, BRO!

Writing a limerick about Yovani Gallardo was challenging.

I'd write one about Yo Gallardo.
I'd have to be more of a bard, though.
I could rhyme Yovani
With Lonny or Donnie.
Hey, this thing is getting quite hard, Bro!

NOT MANFRED

34-year-old rookie Brandon Mann was called up from AAA, reminding me of the '60s rock star Manfred Mann.

Our new guy's name is Brandon Mann.
I'll learn it as fast as I can.
I won't call him Manfred,
At least that's my plan for it
Already I'm his biggest fan.

BRANDON'S DEBUT

Amazing, that debut by Brandon!
I'm glad the new guy had a hand in
A major league game.
He's sure not to blame
For the loss. Gotta go now, we're landin'.

THE CRUZIEST

Crowds in Seattle were surprisingly small in May to see a Mariners team having an excellent season.

Is no one a baseball enthusiast?
Perhaps people here are the choosiest.
But their team is contending,
Their pitching is trending,
And their lineup is the Nelson Cruziest.

THE HEX

This limerick about Nelson Cruz got more reaction than any other... by far.

My feelings toward Cruz are complex.

His homers soar several decks.

He's kind and he's shy,

But if he'd caught that fly

We wouldn't still have this damn hex.

ECK THE MENACE

*Dennis Eckersley is one of my all-time favorites...
what style he has!*

A hitter's worst nightmare was Dennis.

To batters, "Eck" was quite a menace.

He closed and he started.

His pitches just darted,

Like Federer's aces in tennis.

MR. TIGER

*Al Kaline of the Tigers was one of the best
players I've ever seen and I love visiting with him
whenever we play in Detroit.*

Of all the right fielders I've seen,

The greatest came up as a teen.

I'm talking Al Kaline.

This phenom could play fine.

A legend still... know what I mean?

YOU CAN'T PREDICT BASEBALL

*On July 28 in Houston, rookie Ariel Jurado made
his second major league start and we beat the
Astros, who had seven-time All-Star Justin
Verlander on the mound.*

You can't predict baseball's our motto.

The proof is Ariel Jurado.

He outpitched an all-star,

Though George hit the ball far.

I say this in truth, not bravado.

ARIEL'S PRIMERA VICTORIA

*After Ariel Jurado of Panama outpitched Justin
Verlander on July 28, and Rougned Odor went 5
for 5 with 2 HR, I tried my hand at writing limericks
in Spanish...*

Estoy muy emocionado

A causa de Ariel Jurado.

Su primera victoria!

El hizo historia!

Yo lo vi. Que afortunado!

Verlander es la gran estrella,

Y su esposa no es fea.

Hoy, Ariel mejor

Y tambien Odor.

De esto no tuve idea.

HALL OF FAME CLASS 2018

The Hall of Fame vote was intensive.

The Class of '18 is extensive.

Some played years ago

When paychecks were low,

While others were far more expensive.

As dominating as a pharaoh,

Now that was the great Vlad Guerrero.

He thrilled us in '10.

For years before then

He made Wash tear out all his hair though.

There's Chipper, whose name's really Larry.

A guy you'd want your kid to marry.

And you'd call on Trevor,

The best closer ever,

To strike out big sluggers like Barry.

I ask you what did Morris lack

For Cooperstown all those years back?

Was it really a sin

That all he did was win?

If you don't know, you don't know Jack!

Jim Thome hit 600 dingers

And Trammell had very sure fingers.

We honor them all

With plaques at the Hall

So that their sweet legacy lingers.

EMBARRASS THE ASTROS

On July 27, the Rangers beat the first-place Astros after losing 12 of the first 16 games between the clubs. The score was 11-2.

It's nice to embarrass the Astros,

'Cause most of the time they just trash foes.

We love to defeat 'em

And even mistreat 'em

Like Cubans would do to the Castros.

ELIEZER'S SHORT STAY

Eliezer Alvarez was called up by the Rangers for one day, did not get into a game, then was sent back to the minors.

Eliezer was here for a day,

Which seems like a very short stay.

He received a remittance,

Far more than a pittance,

Without even having to play!

REBUILDING

With the Rangers now in rebuilding mode, we wonder...

Can our team rebuild like the Astros,

Who long have forgotten their past woes?

For six years they stunk

And their fan base had shrunk.

Now Minute Maid's full to the last rows.

NO VOTTO

Renato Nunez was claimed on waivers from the A's, but did not play well and was soon released.

We didn't see much of Renato.

What we saw just wasn't that hot though.

While he plays with no fear

At this point it is clear

That he doesn't remind you of Votto.

A GIANT IN CLEATS

2017 Rookie of the Year Aaron Judge is probably the largest major leaguer ever.

Aaron Judge… the giant in cleats,

With quite a collection of feats.

Yes, he made his mark in

"The Apple" by parkin'

A whole lot of balls in the seats.

SLANTIN' PITCHES

2017 MLB Home Run champion
Giancarlo Stanton of the Yankees
is another huge man.

When pitching to Giancarlo Stanton,
Your pitches had better be slantin'.
He's so big, strong and tall,
That if he played football,
He'd likely be enshrined in Canton.

SPECIAL THREADS

All MLB teams wear special patriotic-themed
uniforms on the 4th of July. They all look
surprisingly similar.

Special threads on the 4th of July
Are a great idea but I ask why
Do all of the teams
Look the same (so it seems)?
Can't we be more creative ? Or try ?

NICKNAMES

One listener complained about our using
nicknames for Rangers players.

We've heard what you think about nicknames,
That using them's one of our sick games.
I think players earn 'em,
But you say "just burn 'em".
We'll just toss them all into thick flames.

I hear that the shortened name "Izzy"
Is making you suddenly dizzy.
And our saying "Guzy"
Is making you woozy.
You must not be terribly busy!

Nicknames help make the game flow,
Like Jurickson Profar as Pro.
Now who made you the ref? Uh,
Was it Kiner-Falefa?
Perhaps you should just let it go.

CAN'T BEAT BARTOLO

One bright spot in the Rangers' season was Bartolo "Big Sexy" Colon.

The pitcher Big Sexy Colon

Was so good that hitters would moan,

"All our homers are solo,

We can't beat Bartolo!"

This truth was repeatedly shown.

PASSING JUAN

Juan Marichal was the all-time leading winner from the Dominican Republic going into the season, with Bartolo close behind.

The Dominican star Marichal

Had the highest leg kick of them all.

When Bartolo amasses

More wins and then passes

Him, Cooperstown will want the ball.

HERE COMES BARTOLO

Bartolo Colon eventually passed Juan Marichal as the winningest pitcher ever from the Dominican Republic.

The high-kicking Juan Marichal

Has a plaque with his name in the Hall.

Now here comes Big Bart

Tearing Juan's mark apart.

Maybe someday he too gets the call.

NEXT UP FOR BARTOLO

Next up on Bartolo's list was "El Presidente"
Dennis Martinez, the all-time leader in wins by a
pitcher born in Latin America.

El Presidente is the leader.

He once had a dominant heater.

Now here comes Bartolo,

Who sure throws the ball slow.

Now this will be great baseball theater!

SIXTH TIME THE CHARM?

Passing Marichal made him the all-time leading
winner from the Dominican Republic. Would
Bartolo pass Martinez to become the all-time
winner from Latin America, as well?

This was Bartolo's sixth outing,

With hopes of Dominicans shouting.

After one of these starts

This record will be Bart's,

But I know some of you are now doubting.

BARTOLO TRANQUILO

Colon faced the Mariners ace,

Resuming his historic chase.

Despite some low velo,

Bart sure stayed "tranquilo,"

And now he's the one in first place.

THE SWITCH PITCHER

One of my favorite players is the ambidextrous pitcher Pat Venditte, who pitched for the Dodgers this year.

Whenever they need Pat Venditte,

His left arm and right arm are ready.

He brings the team extras

'Cause he's ambidextrous.

With which hand does he eat spaghetti?

THE FREAK

The Rangers signed "The Freak" Tim Lincecum to a minor league contract but he was released without ever making it up up to the big leagues.

We're sorry we won't see The Freak.

They say that his velo was weak.

I sure hope that he signs

With a new team and finds

He's not totally up the creek.

LEONYS' VOICE

Outfielder Leonys Martin has the most distinctive voice in baseball.

Former Ranger Leonys Martin

Could be heard long before he was seen.

His ladylike voice

Was a curse, not a choice.

And sounded like he was pre-teen.

BAD STARTS AND BODY PARTS

A Rangers-Tigers game featured two starters who were having major control issues.

Fulmer and Moore had bad starts.

In fact, Fulmer was off the charts.

He couldn't throw strikes

And at times we said "Yikes!

He's endangering our body parts!"

SCIOSCIA'S SCOWL

The senior manager in MLB is Mike Scioscia of the Angels. He never looks happy.

The scowl you'll be seeing is Scioscia's.

It makes him look somewhat ferocious.

He's now past Lasorda

In wins, so he oughta

Be thankful he was so precocious.

HAMELS AND HAMMEL

A broadcasters' nightmare was the matchup of Cole Hamels and Jason Hammel of KC.

On Sunday, it's Hamels and Hammel.
I'd just as soon French kiss a camel.
I wish that KC
Would pitch Kennedy.
I'm glad they do not have Ben Gamel.

Hamels-Hammel was Cole versus Jason
A tough one we knew we'd be facin'.
A bad start for Cole
Put us in a hole.
And most of our hitters were chasin'.

It was Hamels and Hammel again
Until Ned Yost went to the pen.
This time our guy Cole
Played the ace starter role,
His best game since… I don't know when.

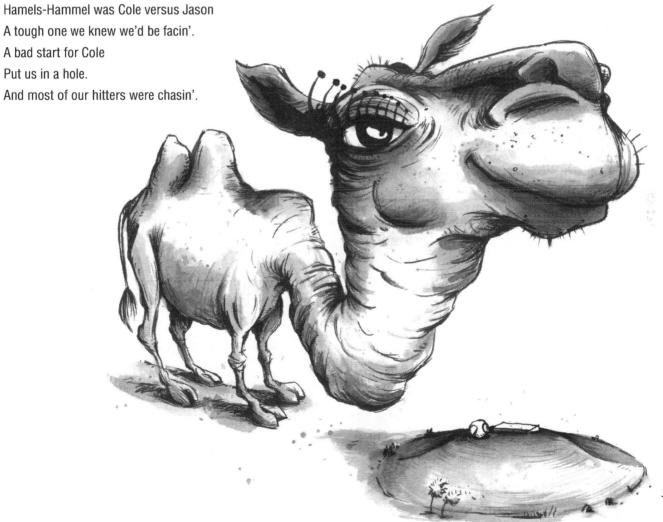

FRIENDLY FENWAY

Although built in 1912, Fenway Park is still a huge thrill to work in.

At Fenway, you know there's a wall.

Thirty-seven feet high, yeah, it's tall.

Sluggers like Yaz and Rice

Didn't treat it so nice.

By denting it hard with the ball.

The fans keep on streaming to Fenway.

To see Alex Cora's best ten play.

Every game is sold out.

Those left out, I'm told pout.

It's amazing the prices that men pay.

PYROTECHNICS

Fireworks nights are still the most popular among fans.

The nights we are always promoting
Have big pyrotechnics exploding.
For fans of fireworks
There are no higher perks
In the park, at the yard, or while boating.

TAGGER SWAGGER

Rougned Odor has a special flair when he tags out runners.

We think Rougie is the best tagger.
He does it with a special swagger.
He tags those runners out
Without leaving a doubt,
And prances around like Mick Jagger.

A'S BLAZE

In mid-June, the Oakland A's were 12 games behind Houston. On August 18th, the A's tied the Astros for first place.

The team on fire now is the A's.
Can Texas extinguish their blaze?
It looks like Team Astro
Is now a disastro.
The A's all look like Willie Mays.

ONE FINE ATHLETIC

The Rangers cannot get Khris Davis out, regardless of what kind of slump he may be in.

Khris Davis is one fine Athletic
But lately his bat's been pathetic.
If the pitcher's a Ranger
Then Khris is a danger
And all with him is copasetic.

GIVE US A BREAK, KHRIS

On back-to-back days in July, Davis hit game-winning homers at Texas.

I don't know how much more I can take.
Now it's Jose, Keone and Jake.
This fellow Khris Davis
Will surely enslave us.
Now would someone please give us a break?

LEFT MY HEART AT AT&T

AT&T Park in San Francisco is the most unique park in baseball, with McCovey Cove, the Coke Bottle, The Glove, Renell the PA announcer, and old guys serving as Ball Dudes.

We love it at AT&T,
A prettier park you won't see.
While Coors has the mountains
And Kauffman has fountains,
This may be the best of the three.

There's a glove and a bottle of Coke.
To hit them would take a long poke.
You likely can tell
The voice here's Renell,
A woman! No, that is no joke.

Now nothing enhances my mood
Like watching a senior "ball dude,"
Or a pretty brunette
Serving as a dudette.
(I hope that I'm not being rude.)

The longest home runs make a splash.
Those drives leave the park in a flash.
The fans in a boat
Hope that baseballs do float.
Home run balls can bring lots of cash.

BRONX BOMBERS

The Yankees set a new team home run record despite losing Aaron Judge and Gary Sanchez for lengthy stretches due to injury. Obviously, home run-friendly Yankee Stadium's dimensions have something to do with this.

The Yanks set a new home run mark
As balls just fly out of their park.
They miss Judge and Gary,
But drives have such carry
Both in day games and after dark.

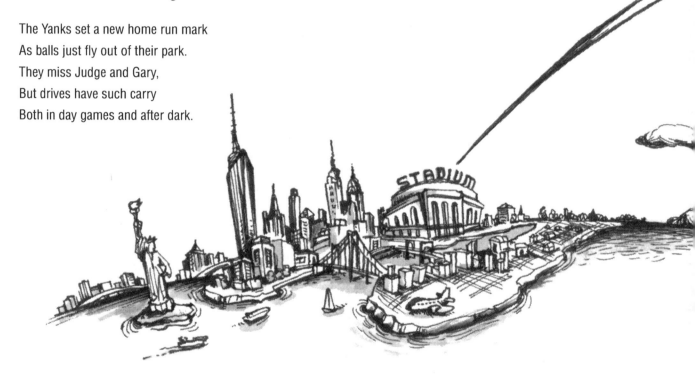

They might not have Mantle and Maris,
But they have the guns to embarrass
The opposing teams' staffs,
When all their pitching gaffes
Are launched half the distance to Paris.

37

MILK AND COOKIES

The Yankees surprisingly had the youngest lineup in the American League.

The Yankees have several young rookies.

It's making things tough on the bookies.

Torres and Andujar

Can hit the ball too far

For kids who should eat milk and cookies.

FINALLY THE TWINS

The Rangers didn't play the Twins until June 21.

We're finally playing the Twins,
Whose season has not been all grins.
"Contenders" they're labeled
But stars are disabled.
They're way behind Cleveland in wins.

To Cleveland, they're second banana.
But soon they'll have Earvin Santana.
And maybe Sano
But you never know.
Don't write it in your weekly plannah.

VERLANDER CANDOR

Justin Verlander of the Astros had a super-human season at the age of 35.

The numbers for Justin Verlander
Are awesome, I say in all candor.
Perhaps it is Kate
Or maybe just fate.
They're Gibson-like. Just take a gander.

How can a guy Verlanders' age
Get better at this advanced stage?
Perhaps a new pine tar?
(I heard at a wine bar.)
Or maybe it's uncontrolled rage.

MAUER POWER

Joe Mauer is one of my favorites, but many Twins fans feel his long-term contract has tied the hands of the team's management.

I hope Twins fans don't hate Joe Mauer.
I know that his contract is sour.
He still has the strokes
For the singles he pokes.
He just doesn't have any power.

MINOR DETAIL

Mike Minor was the Rangers' leading winner and fortunately under club control for two more years.

The season is now halfway done,
With many more games lost than won.
During this second half
We might trade half our staff.
The chance we trade Mike Minor: none.

THE CATCH

Gary Matthews Jr. was the Rangers Player of the Year in 2006 and made the greatest catch I've ever seen. It was great to see him when he broadcast a Rangers game in Oakland in August.

We're happy to see GMJ.
He made that remarkable play.
It was crushed by Mike Lamb...
Gary leaped, said, "No ma'am",
Caught it and we shouted, "Say hey!"

In center field, he was a glider.
He moved like a player much lighter.
His climb of the wall
Was the greatest of all
And truly resembled a spider.

The catch was in 2006,
And Gary had many more tricks.
He hit for the cycle
And outperformed Michael,
Attracting a bevy of chicks.

SPEED IT UP!

I believe that speeding up the pace of the game is baseball's biggest challenge.

We better speed up pace of play,
'Cause fans aren't willing to stay.
Either go to the pitch clock
Or else, as in Hitchcock
Films, they'll all be frightened away.

The mound visit limit helps some,
Although most of you thought it was dumb.
When players and coaches
Converge there like roaches,
What should I do, just suck my thumb?

TALKING MIKE

On August 3rd, the Rangers gave away a talking microphone featuring some of my best-liked radio calls and we promoted it for two weeks.

The Eric Nadel talking mike

Is something I hope you will like.

In ways it will tease you,

Perhaps it will please you,

But it might scare your little tyke.

D AS IN DELINO

Rangers center fielder Delino Deshields was leading MLB in many defensive categories, including difficult catches.

Perhaps you will think I'm a wino.

But no one's as good as Delino.

Four-star catches and fives

Running down those long drives,

He's making the other team cry, "NO!"

ROUGIE ON FIRE

After a terrible start, Rougned Odor went on a hot streak beginning in May and got even hotter as July turned to August.

It's amazing how Rougned Odor

Had a start that was dreadfully poor.

But now he's on fire.

Can he go any higher?

(His contract's not bad anymore.)

He used to be known for the punch

That made Jose B spit his lunch.

Now his bat is speaking.

I think that he's peaking.

His home runs have come in a bunch.

TRAPEZOID

*The Mariners used a four-man trapezoid defense
on the right side of the field against Joey Gallo.*

The M's employ a trapezoid

Against Joe so they can avoid

A hard hit to right.

Now, night after night,

I bet Joey's getting annoyed.

GO DEEP GALLO

On May 15 in Seattle, Joey Gallo helped send the game into extra innings. We hoped he would end the game, too.

Into extras the game would continue

Thanks to Gallo and his mighty sinew.

Okay, Mr. Gallo,

Go deep! Don't go shallow.

We know that you have it within you.

VICTORY OR TRICKERY?

The Rangers emerged from a long funk with three straight wins in late May.

We're hoping for a third straight victory.
It sure looks like something has clicked, you see.
Could three nights of winning
Foreshadow beginning
Of solid play? Or just some trickery?

NATIONAL TEQUILA DAY

On July 24, the A's came back from a 10-2 deficit to beat the Rangers. It happened to be National Tequila Day.

On National Tequila Day,
The A's just would not go away.
We were leading by eight,
But then lost the game late.
Do I need a shot? Well, I may.

HARD FEELINGS

An incident at second base between Rougned Odor and Andrelton Simmons caused some very hard feelings between the Rangers and Angels.

Will Anaheim throw at Odor,
Since Andrelton Simmons is sore?
Remember Bautista
Got knocked on his keister.
Did that really even the score?

It seems cooler heads will prevail,
But is that the end of this tale?
We're back in September
And players remember
These bench clearing things without fail.

TRADE RUMORS

It's not quite as bad as a tumor
When someone creates a trade rumor.
Some of these creations
Could cause palpitations,
Unless you have a sense of humor.

CHOO CHOO TRAIN

Shin-Soo Choo broke Julio Franco's Texas Rangers' record 46-game   on base streak.

Choo's record streak's now 47.
He sure has his hit engine revvin'.
He's now surpassed Julio,
Who once had an awesome "fro".
And all others, even Phil Nevin.

CHOO'S DRIVE

Shin-Soo Choo eventually ran his club record on base streak to 52 games.

Shin-Soo Choo at the top, he is streaking,

Which is good 'cause the offense was leaking.

Now Choo's thirty-five

But he still has the drive

To excel, and right now he is peaking.

NO CLOCK CLEANING

The White Sox swept the Rangers in Chicago in mid-May, with all three games being close.

Three close games were lost to the Sox...

Another of this season's shocks.

The run differential

Was inconsequential.

At least they did not clean our clocks.

FROZEN CLOSER

The White Sox were having another rough year. Their bullpen was especially problematic.

With the White Sox, I don't know who's closin'.

Depends on which day he is chosen.

They've had so much bad weather,

I just hope that whenever

They have a lead, he's not half frozen!

BIRTHDAY SHOTS

May 16 is a birthday I share with Rangers pitching coach Doug Brocail and Equipment Manager Brandon Boyd.

Since this is my actual b-day,

I hope you will give me some leeway.

Both Brandon and Broke

Will be in on the joke

When the tray of shots is split up three-way.

TOO MUCH CAFFEINE

The Rangers make three trips a year to Seattle to play the Mariners, long time Rangers rivals.

The ballpark here's spotlessly clean

And the fans in Seattle ain't mean.

But the games make me nervous.

Perhaps it's Scott Servais,

Or maybe it's too much caffeine!

VEECK'S LEGACY

The exploding scoreboard at Chicago's Guaranteed Rate Field is the legacy of former Sox owner Bill Veeck.

Chicago's scoreboard is exploding.

This was Bill Veeck's style of promoting.

Bill's basic intention:

A major invention

Like the rigged machines they used for voting.

NUN IN A BAR

On May 12, the Astros beat the Rangers despite a Ronald Guzman home run.
Astros DH Evan Gattis stole a base... just the third of his big league career.

This game is already bizarre.

Our Guzman hit one really far.

Gattis stole one off Fister.

I'm telling you, Mister...

That's as rare as a nun in a bar!

PLUNKED BY WITCHES

On June 9, Astros pitchers hit six Rangers batters.

Six Ranger guys were hit by pitches.

How evil! (as if done by witches).

Only one of them scored,

Others were left on board.

An unfulfilled bundle of riches.

CUBBIE COLE

On July 26, the Rangers traded Cole Hamels to the Cubs, making him the sixth former Ranger on their pitching staff.

The Rangers have now traded Cole.
For two years he played the "ace" role.
We twice won the West
But you know all the rest.
Lately he's put us in a hole.

Of course Cole has gone to the Cubs,
Not one of the eight other clubs.
He's their sixth former Ranger
So he won't be a stranger.
He'll now buy their drinks at the pubs.

SCOUTING COLE

With trade rumors swirling, Cole Hamels had a very poor outing against the A's.

A rather large number of scouts
Were here to see Cole record outs.
A nightmarish second
Did not help, I reckon,
To end any lingering doubts.

59

WILL JD TRADE KEONE?

One of the big questions leading up to the July 31 trade deadline was whether Keone Kela would be traded.

Will J.D. trade Keone Kela?

He's one mighty valuable fellah.

I hope that Keone

Brings back a Jim Thome,

Or maybe a Roy Campanella.

JAKE THE SNAKE

In Phoenix on July 31, the Rangers traded Jake Diekman to the Diamonbacks.

We had a great three years with Jake.

Not one thing about him is fake.

Without part of his colon,

This whole year he's been rollin'.

In Phoenix he's now "Jake the Snake."

WHAT'S NEW?

Jeff Banister was fired on Sept. 21st and Don Wakamatsu became the Rangers' Interim Manager. Getting home runs from Beltre and Gallo, the Rangers beat the Mariners in a rain-shortened game, 8-3.

I got to the park and asked, "What's new?"

The answer was Don Wakamatsu.

The interim skipper

Is usually chipper.

I just hope he knows what to not do.

The Rangers came up with some runs,

A couple of threes, not just ones.

Hard rain was approaching

And soon was encroaching.

Good thing they wheeled out the big guns.

CAN WE SAY HABOOB?

On July 30 in Phoenix, we had a 22-minute power outage and were knocked off the air due to a dust and wind storm called a haboob.

We lost power due to haboob.

(Can we say that word on the tube?)

We lost our connection

In every section.

Perhaps some key part needed lube?

BOCHY'S CALM

I really admire Giants manager Bruce Bochy. His expression never changes. He's always calm, at least on the outside.

The Giants won three series rings,

But different results this year brings.

Bruce Bochy's demeanor

Is kinder, not meaner.

Is that man immune to mood swings?

"THE WAY BASEBALL GO"

Wash says, "That's the way baseball go."

We won't be in this year's fall show.

One day we'll be in it

And then when we win it,

I'll make that last call nice and slow.

NOT BASEBALL

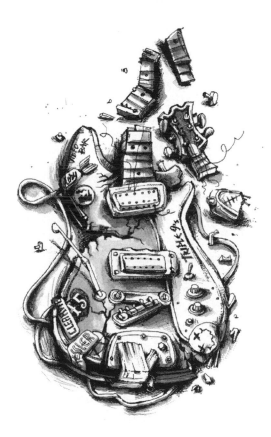

WORLD CUP PREVIEW

My broadcast partners, Matt and Jared, are both huge soccer fans and challenged me to write a World Cup preview limerick, using all 32 teams.

Now who will win this year's World Cup?
I've wondered since I was a pup.
Now could it be Portugal
Or have they no chance at all?
Argentina! (If they don't "mess up.")

So many are betting on Spain,
The obvious choice in my brain.
The chance we were seekin'
Went to Costa Ricans,
Which left an indelible stain.

There's always a chance that Brazil
Can channel Pele and then thrill.
It could be the Germans,
Who don't like Trump's sermons.
They've already climbed the big hill.

World Cup hope for most is remote.
They're all in the same hopeless boat.
It won't be the home team,
As Russia's long odds seem
So bad one cannot sugarcoat.

And as for the Belgians from Brussels,
They're favored in most of their tussles.
If you picked Croatia
You need euthanasia.
Australians drink beer and eat mussels.

I love that the Cup has Egyptians.
If they win, we'll all have conniptions.
Denmark sends out Danes.
"Not great", one complains,
Unless they have real good prescriptions!

Poland's chances to look good are over
(Except Paulina Porizkova).
Iceland could sneak in.
We'd all be freakin',
Like 2016 Villanova.

Could champ of this tourney be Sweden?
In their group, they're sure to be beaten.
The French have been missing…
(They're too busy kissing.)
And England might win…if it's cheatin'.

Can Mexico scale the big wall
And capture the Cup after all?
The Swiss will be tying.
"They're neutral!" we're crying.
And give me a break: Senegal?

I'm partial a bit to Peru.
Colombia speaks Spanish, too.
As do Panamanians,
Instead of Canadians.
Morocco has some Spaniards, too.

So Uruguay's star Luis Suarez
Produces like young Gleyber Torres.
But he's known to bite,
And start the odd fight,
Like drunk college students in Juarez.

I've written a couple of blurbs
Without ever touting the Serbs.
Now how 'bout Tunisia?
Would their winning please ya?
These two sides would need special herbs!

A long shot is the Japanese.
And Saudi Arabia? Please!
Maybe South Korea,
If bad diarrhea
Hits all of the foes that it sees.

Nigeria's last in this poem.
They just never entered my dome.
And for those that don't win,
Let's relieve their chagrin
By giving them cups made of chrome.

WORLD CUP SEMI-FINALS

In the semi-finals, France knocked off Belgium and Croatia upset England.

So now it's the French and Croatians.
They stand above all other nations.
It was no one's prediction.
It seemed much like fiction.
(The other teams all on vacation.)

Congratulations to Croatia.
Where are you? In Europe or Asia?
At 35-1,
We thought your chance was none.
And now the French side has to face ya.

WHAT'S CROATIA LIKE?

Everyone wanted to know about Croatia. What's it like there? So, I did some research...

Croatia has more than one island

And coastline. But what about high land?

If you ask a Cro-at.

"Hey dude, where's the snow at?"

He'll likely be laughin' and smilin'.

WORLD CUP FINAL

In the final, France defeated the dark horse Croatian team.

The World Cup belongs now to France.

The whole country's doing a dance.

No more midfielders flopping,

Champagne corks are popping,

I hope no one's wetting their pants.

Too bad the World Cup's not Croatia's.

The way they hung in was bodacious.

They impressed on the pitch,

All their names end in "ich"!

What a fabulous run... Goodness Gracious!

VIKINGS' NEW DOME

Minneapolis replaced the horrible Metrodome with two great stadiums, Target Field and US Bank Stadium, both of which look very unique.

The Vikings' new dome, "US Bank"…

Imposing it is, to be frank.

It's a much nicer home

Than the old Metrodome,

Which really, you know, kind of stank.

BULLSEYE!

The Target sign at Target Field drives me insane as the dog's tail wags at me all game.

The Target dog's wagging its tail…

I love it, but wish it would fail.

It's in our line of sight

Catching my eye all night.

If I break it, please pay my bail!

TREES AND BREEZE

Seattle is my favorite city in the US... I wrote multiple limericks about it.

Seattle has stores that sell weed.

It's legal, if that's what you need.

There are mountains and trees

And a nice ocean breeze.

Does anyone stay home and read?

UMBRELLA

I especially love Safeco Field because the retractable roof does not enclose the stadium, it just protects it from rain.

The roof really is an umbrella.

That it's not connected is stellar.

I'm anticipating

That soon I'll be stating,

"The save goes to Keone Kela."

SAFECO FIELD

In Seattle, the ballpark is far

From our hotel but don't send a car.

I like walking to Safeco.

It's two miles. My legs chafe though.

I need lubricant. Bring me a jar!

NO BASKETBALL!

Two of Seattle's announcers were injured in a pick-up basketball game and had to miss games.

The Seattle announcers are bold,

But they need to accept that they're old.

Rizzs and Simsie blew out

And there's really no doubt

That "No basketball!" they should be told.

KC BBQ

Kansas City BBQ runs the gamut, from barely OK to sublime... I tend to eat too much.

The BBQ here is diverse.
It hardly fits in just one verse.
We love Q39
And Gates sauce is divine.
Eat more, and we'll leave in a hearse!

BALTIMORE BEST BITES

A listener asked for my dining recommendations in Baltimore.

For lunch, you should go to Miss Shirley.
It's best to go late, or real early.
And you'll enjoy greatly
The crab cakes at Faidley,
Although service there can be surly.

ERIC NADEL'S DAY OFF

Union Square in San Francisco is one of my favorite places to hang out.

There's lots to see in Union Sguare.
It's hard to not stand there and stare.
There's a mime and lounge singer.
Where's my wife? Did I bring her?
I wish I'd remembered a chair.

The square is remarkably clean.
A movie plays on a big screen.
They show Ferris Bueller.
Now what could be cooler?
Wish I'd been like him as a teen.

NATIONAL LIMERICK DAY

Saturday, May 12 is National Limerick Day, prompting multiple limericks in honor of the occasion.

It's National Limerick Day,

Just perfect for us you might say.

We'll whip out some verse

For better or worse

So listeners won't go away.

DAPHNE

This one is for my dear friend, the amazingly talented Daphne Willis.

On Limerick Day, this is for Daphne

Not a day with her is ever laugh-free.

How all this came about,

I can't figure it out.

Perhaps it is half her and half me.

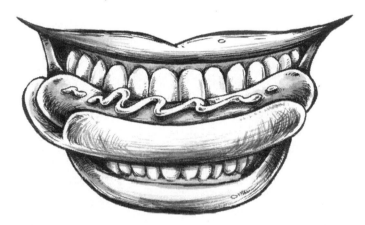

FREQUENT LIMERICKS

On National Limerick Day

The Rangers and Astros will play.

If the game starts to suck

Then you're really in luck.

Frequent limericks will then be OK.

EATING CHAMPS

On July 4, Joey Chestnut and Miki Sudo successfully defended their Nathan's Hot Dog Eating Contest championship in Coney Island.

The women's champ is Miki Sudo

(Of eating, not tennis or judo).

And again Joey Chestnut

Proved he has the best gut.

Ate 74... Does he chew, though?

MY FAVORITE VENUES

The best place for concerts is Red Rocks...
For everyone, crew cuts or dreadlocks.
The breathtaking setting
Is best, I am betting.
Not going there should earn you head knocks.

In Dallas, the Kessler's the place.
It's truly a magical space.
With perfect acoustics,
No juke box, no cue sticks.
It just puts a smile on my face.

I once went to Carnegie Hall,
The most famous venue of all.
I saw Mahavishnu
Orchestra and wish you
Could go there soon... maybe this fall?

So many more venues abound,
And some of them I haven't found.
Although I can't mention
Them all, my intention
Is find those that have the best sound.

MY HOME AWAY FROM HOME

The Kessler at first was Gene Autry's.
But then it just rotted and caught fleas.
The neighborhood faced
This incredible waste.
Then Edwin said, "Can it be bought, please?"

He made it a fabulous showplace.
For rockers and those with a slow pace.
That low hanging balcony
Is now like a pal to me.
A better room you will find ...no place.

He brilliantly brought in Jeff Liles
To find the best acts of all styles.
Blues bands and folk singers
And Singapore Slingers.
The audience leaves here with smiles.

In Houston we now have The Heights.
Bands play there too and don't need flights.
From what I can figure
The Houston room's bigger
Both theaters are historic sites.

NBA FINALS

*We watched the Warriors eliminate the Rockets
in the NBA semi-finals, prompting this one.*

The finals have Cav vs War.

The Warriors showed Houston the door

'Cause the Rockets went frigid

Like the rim was too rigid.

We've all seen this matchup before.

FC DALLAS

*If you haven't seen our professional soccer team
play at Toyota Stadium, it's well worth the trip.*

We're lucky to have FC Dallas.

Their home field in Frisco's a palace.

Their parking is easy,

The fans aren't sleazy,

Hope they win that MLS chalice.

TALL GIRLS

*I love women's basketball and wish I could go
to more games, but their season is the same time
as ours.*

Dallas Wings, you are talented tall girls.

You have better hands even than ball girls.

You can drive, jump and shoot…

I hope you win the loot

When you play for the title this fall, girls.

VEGAS KNIGHTS

The most amazing sports story of the year was the expansion Vegas Knights going all the way to the Stanley Cup Finals, only to lose to the Capitals on Memorial Day.

Vegas Knights can provide this tutorial,

Without being too professorial,

That players rejected

And left unprotected

Can win on this Monday Memorial.

MATT IN PADS

My broadcast partner Matt Hicks is a lifelong Washington Capitals fan and vowed to broadcast an entire Rangers game in hockey shoulder pads if the Caps actually won the Cup. Of course, they did. And Matt lived up to his promise.

In Hell, it has never been colder.

Matt's Caps won the Cup! Since he's older,

There'd be no need to hide

If he broke down and cried.

Instead he wore pads on his shoulder.

SWEATY SHOULDERS

After I posted my limerick about Matt in shoulder pads, he responded with this one:

It's certain those pads made me sweat.

Up North, I might say, "Je suis pret"

To do what I'm able

And bring to the table

A love for my team sans regret.

DEPENDING ON RHYME

My love of writing limericks fascinates me. I have written many about the passion and the process.

The limerick depends on its rhyme,
Which comes easily not all the time.
They can be quite a stretch,
Making everyone wretch.
Other times, they can be quite sublime.

CHEAP TRICK

Writing limericks: a cheap little trick,
Maybe something of which you are sick.
But this little rhyme
Helps me pass the time
And I think it's now part of my shtick.

BORED LISTENERS

Although I've won Ford Frick's Award,
I fear that our listeners get bored.
I hope writing in verse
Doesn't take bad to worse,
But last time I read one, they roared.

ADDICTION

So this limerick thing's an addiction,
But it's really a harmless affliction.
It's not easy to stop
Writing this crazy slop.
We'll keep writing them. That's my prediction.

INTERVENTION

It looks like I need an intervention.
It would help achieve limerick prevention.
If I write just one more
They'll toss me in the door
Of the senior men's house of detention.

RE-ARRANGED MIND

Sometimes I wake up in the middle of the night with limericks in my head. My mind is altered... this, when a friend of mine tried to convince me otherwise.

So you really don't think I have changed…

That my mind has not been re-arranged?

I can't think without trying

A rhyme, else I'm crying.

I believe I'm completely deranged!

CHIPOTLE

Food on our charter flights can be hit or miss...

The food on the plane's from Chipotle.

It's better than going by boat, see?

It's a four hour flight,

Most of it in daylight.

I might just get drunk, but don't quote me!

FLY ON THE WALL

A friend challenged me to speak in limericks for a whole day, as long as she got to follow me around.

Yeah, you'd be a fly on the wall,

And I'd be the weirdest of all.

With all my words rhymin'

I'm hardly Paul Simon

And don't have Garfunkel to call!

SPINNING BASEBALL TUNES

KXT 91.7 is my favorite radio station. They invited me to do a one hour DJ set, playing only songs about baseball.

I'm on KXT Friday with Amy

Playing DJ for free. (They don't pay me.)

Baseball songs on the menu.

Just tune in and then you

Will understand why. Can you blame me?

I know a song 'bout Joltin' Joe.

They played in the '50s, you know.

On Friday at noon

I'll play you this tune,

And one that's called, "Go Ichiro!"

NELSON OR TED?

A twitter follower thought my Nelson Cruz limerick referred to Ted Cruz.

Oh, you thought I meant Senator Cruz?

Politics... not a subject I choose.

Though it was my major

In college, I'd wager

That now, it just gives me the blues.

THE WALL

Canada legalized marijuana beginning in the fall of 2018.

Canada will need a wall

More than a hundred feet tall

To keep out our stoners,

(Some social, some loners),

Because weed there's legal this fall.

FREEWAY ANXIETY

*LA Freeways can have very short on-ramps... much
too short! And with far too many trucks.*

It's awful when your rental car sucks

On freeways out here that don't bar trucks.

To avoid getting hurt

You had best stay alert,

And better drink plenty of Starbucks!

POET'S DAY

Every year, August 21 is Poet's Day, dedicated to the "crafters of poetry."

This day honors every last poet,

A special day… hope I don't blow it!

Will some extra rhyming

Throw off all our timing?

If so, hope our broadcast won't show it.

Now being a crafter of verse

Is not just a gift… but a curse?

This cool rhyming tendency

Becomes a dependency.

I guess there are traits that are worse.

Both Dickinson and Allan Poe

Were young when their time came to go.

But Whitman and Frost

Were old when they crossed

And so was Maya Angelou.

SUMMER READING

I'm honored to be the chairman of the Texas Rangers Summer Reading Club.

It's time to do our summer reading,

A great program that children are needing.

These kids have a burning

Desire for learning.

That's the hunger that we should be feeding!

WRECK-FREE DRIVING

Writing limericks to friends on their birthday saves money on cards.

A big happy birthday to Lexie.

I hope that your big day is wreck-free.

Beer glasses are clinking

But please don't be drinking

And driving, 'cause cops gonna check pee!

MOTHER'S DAY

Mother's Day... the perfect time for limericks!

I forgot that this day is for mother.

I don't have one, not even a brother.

But regardless of day,

What I would like to say

Is let's all just take care of each other.

MY SISTER LAURIE

My sister Laurie is a talented writer and always stands up for her beliefs.

I'm so proud of my sister Laur.

She taught me what ideals are for.

She's always protested

The things she's detested.

I wish I could see her some more.

THE VOICE OF YANKEE STADIUM

Paul Olden has been the PA voice of the new Yankee Stadium since it opened in 2009.

To follow Bob Sheppard in here

Was tough 'cause that man had no peer.

But somehow Paul Olden,

With his voice that's golden,

Has showered the fans with good cheer.

DAPHNE AND BNL AT LEVITT

Levitt Pavilion, the amazing outdoor music venue in Arlington, announced an end of season show featuring two of my all-time favorites, Daphne Willis and Barenaked Ladies.

Daphne and Barenaked Ladies…

Better than even the Sadies!

I've seen both before,

Fifteen times or more

So better stay out of my way please.

It's Daphne and Barenaked Ladies

At Levitt. They don't often play these.

The band and the artist

I think are the smartest!

I can't wait for photos, so say "Cheese!"

Who's gonna see Barenaked Ladies?

Eight hundred say yes, and six maybes.

"If I Had a Million…"

At Levitt Pavilion!

I just hope it's not hot as Hades.

ALL-STARS

MY FAVORITE BANDS

My favorite rock band is E Street.
I see them and then want a repeat.
I've idolized Springsteen
Since he was a string bean.
For my money those guys can't be beat.

My number two fave was Tom Petty.
I'd bounce around 'til I was sweaty.
Some bands are just fakers,
But not the Heartbreakers.
Tom's gone now and we were not ready.

My main man from Dallas is Rhett.
He hits the stage like a small jet.
An Old 97
Since he was 11.
(Or something like that, I forget!)

I will see the Eagles one day.
I'm finally willing to pay
Big bucks to see Henley.
(I'd like to be friendly
With him as he lives out my way.)

I never have seen Stevie Wonder.
Can't tell you what rock I was under.
Since I was 16,
He's been part of my scene.
Not seeing him has been a blunder.

Those are just a few of my faves.
And new bands keep coming in waves.
Those brilliant musicians,
Not unlike magicians,
Perform the tricks that this guy craves.

LAKE STREET DIVE

In 2010, I discovered a band from Boston that was unlike any other I had ever heard.

There's no band quite like Lake Street Dive.
They used to be four, now they're five.
They showed me that isthmus
Rhymes nicely with Christmas
And all this makes me feel alive.

You can't label their musical style.
I've been telling folks that for a while.
Their own songs and some covers
About fiends, friends and lovers,
Make me marvel at them and just smile.

RACHAEL

JULIE

✗ BRIDGET ♥

McDUCK

MIKE

THE INIMITABLE HAWK

White Sox TV announcer Hawk Harrelson is one of my all-time favorites and one of the all-time characters. 2018 was his farewell year.

The White Sox announcer named Hawk
Is one guy I like to hear talk.
But your time's running out
To hear that cool shout,
"He gone," because he's gonna walk.

His name's not Hawk, it's really Ken.
I've watched him again and again.
He's one of a kind.
I really don't mind.
That he brazenly roots for his men.

My favorite of his well-known calls…
On a deep drive that hooks and then falls.
Hawk says, "Right size, wrong shape!"
Making listeners gape.
It's reserved for the longest foul balls.

When the Sox as a team really stank,
'Twas Hawk who then nicknamed big Frank.
35 on his shirt,
Hawk said, "Here's the Big Hurt,"
And the big man took that to the bank.

On the air, Hawk's eternally friendly.
Which these days just isn't a trend, see?
He works with Steve Stone,
(A rock star on his own).
Heck, he'd even work with Bob Brenly.

He should win the award named Ford Frick.
That he hasn't won makes me sick.
Perhaps the past winners
Read this for beginners
And give him the honor real quick.

Goodbye to this man we can learn off,
As he readies to take the next turnoff.
Hope he drops some putts,
And doesn't go nuts,
From draining the planet of Smirnoff.

95

EVERYBODY LOVES EMILY

Emily Jones is the Rangers field reporter and is universally beloved.

We all adore Emily Jones,
Although her bad jokes bring us groans.
In that small camera well,
It can be hot as hell.
Still, her voice has such refreshing tones

She's comfortable in her own skin.
She owns every scene that she's in.
With gentle suggestion,
She'll ask any question.
Just watch after each Rangers win.

She's one of a kind, this Ms. Jones.
Wish she had twin sisters or clones.
Our whole batting order
Is there to support her.
They've ruined every dress that she owns!

THE WRIGHT GIRL

I love Chely Wright, and was determined to get her to play a show at Café Momentum. Somehow my plan worked.

My dream was to get Chely Wright

To play here. (Sometimes I'm not bright.)

So I pitch her Chad Houser,

And somehow that wows her.

I'm proud to present her tonight.

THE INCOMPARABLE RUTHIE FOSTER

Ruthie Foster is one of the unknown superstars of the music business... But this year she won the prestigious Koko Taylor Award for contemporary blues.

Ruthie Foster is getting her due.

Koko Taylor Award made that true.

She deserved this great honor

That they bestowed on her.

She'll sing songs next year in Cuba, too!

WALKER'S STALKER

Seth Walker is one of my favorite singer-songwriters.

This is the amazing Seth Walker.

He's a singer, guitarist and talker.

When I first heard him play,

I could not stay away.

For a while he thought I was a stalker!

BRAD SHAM, THE VOICE OF THE COWBOYS

Brad Sham (who is now in his 40th year as the Dallas Cowboys announcer) and I were partners
for 3 years on Rangers broadcasts in the mid '90s.

I used to be partners with Brad.
He's one of the best that I've had.
We worked exhibitions
With no inhibitions,
Although all the players were bad.

You see, the real guys were on strike.
The owners told them, "Take a hike!"
The team of replacements
Were dug up from basements,
And there we still were at the mike.

When Brad made his first home run call,
We couldn't believe that the ball
Made it out of the yard.
Although it was hit hard,
Nothing else had gone over the wall.

One day, the real players returned.
And in just a short time Brad discerned
That there's too many games,
Unpronouncable names,
And hotel details to be learned.

Well that's when his pal Jerry Jones
Got on one of his telephones
He brought back the voice.
Who was all the fans' choice.
At least that's one good move he owns!

99

"Brad, thissa Jurry..."

THE RADIO VOICES OF THE YANKEES

*John Sterling and Suzyn Waldman are the Yankees'
incomparable broadcast team, and my dear friends.*

I'm a big fan of John and of Suzyn.

I listen to them of my choosin'.

They're never restricted.

I could have predicted

That they'd sound great even when losin'.

They're fabulous… Waldman and Sterling.

I'd listen to them broadcast curling.

In each Yankees season,

They're the voice of reason,

Even when rumors are swirling.

COOP, THE VOICE OF THE MAVERICKS

Chuck Cooperstein, a native New Yorker like me, has been radio voice of the Dallas Mavericks for 14 years.

When Chuck was born, some lost stork
Deposited him in New York.
Well, really Long Island,
Which truly is my land,
Except I am more of a dork.

Well, somehow, he wound up in Philly.
In winter, that place is quite chilly!
He came down to our state
Without much on his plate,
A move that some might have termed, "silly."

But now look at how it turned out.
This lifelong Knicks fan got to shout
When the Mavs won the crown.
His great call is renowned.
Now that's what I'm talking about!

I hope that Chuck gets to call more
Before he gets pushed out the door.
I have not had that thrill,
I'm awaiting it still.
Am I jealous? No… just a bit sore.

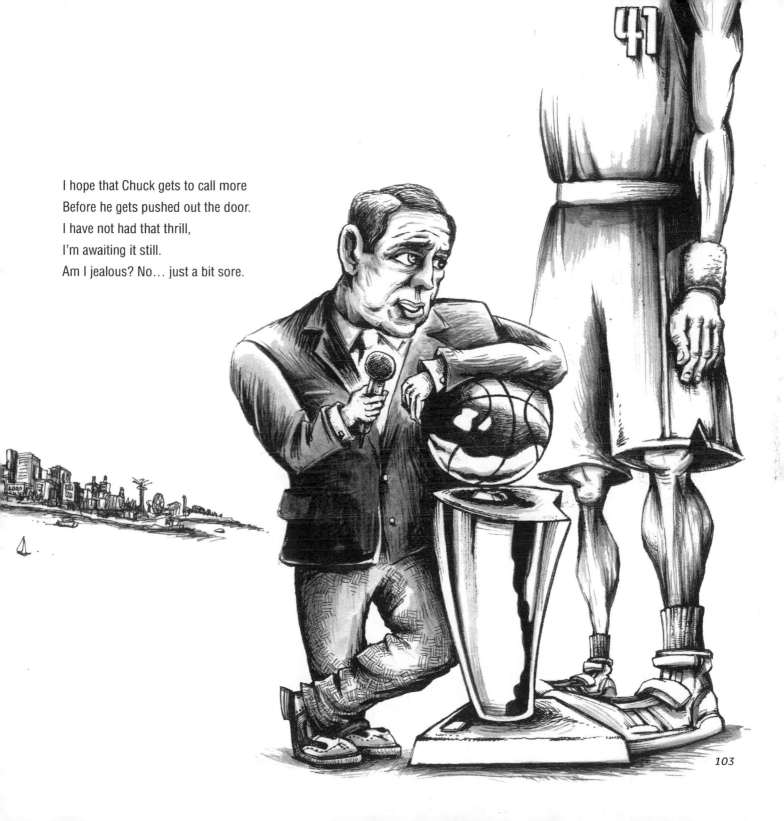

JARED AND EMILY

*My broadcast partner Jared Sandler somehow got
an amazing woman to marry him this month!*

I don't mean to brown nose or pander,
But I am quite proud of young Sandler.
He met this chick Emily.
Soon they'll have a family.
Now how in the world did he land her?

It was love at first sight, I am betting.
She clearly did not do much vetting.
Somehow, he disarmed her
And, clearly, he charmed her.
But I'll believe this at the wedding!

THE MUSERS

The Musers, George Dunham and Craig Miller, have had the top-rated talk show in DFW for years. This year, they were kind enough to serve as moderators for Talk of the Town, the annual charity event that I do with Brad Sham and Chuck Cooperstein.

We're glad we had Dunham and Miller.
Their radio show is a killer.
One plays the guitar,
And one rides his bike far,
We laugh at them like Phyllis Diller.

Now some say the real star is Keith,
Although his name's listed beneath.
Their opinions are hot.
When they take their best shot
They're accurate as Jordan Spieth.

We thought that our chances were slight
That they'd host this. We hoped that they might.
We feared they'd be busy.
We must have been dizzy.
They rarely get asked out at night!

NORM AND DONNIE

*There is no radio program I enjoy being on more than the show hosted
by Norm Hitzges and Donovan Lewis, with Mike Sirois chiming in.*

I love being on air with Norm,

Although he can stir up a storm.

He's never malicious

(He went to Canisius!)

And he's glued to that racing form.

His partner is called Donnie Doo.

Sirois is a funny guy, too.

They both are from Texas.

Their fans are both sexes.

Why this is… I haven't a clue!

THE HARDLINE

I go back to the Zoo days with Rhyner,
Long before he became a Hardliner.
Mike was one funny fellah
With Rhody and Labella.
Morning radio's never been finer.

You know these days his hair is all gray.
That does not mean that Rhyner won't stay.
If he leaves Petty Theft
We would all be bereft.
Hope the Old Wolf ain't going away.

Now someone no doubt will implore me
To write a few lines about Corby.
Mike's partner in crime
Made immortal in rhyme?
Now what could an easier chore be?

Some were thinking their show would lose glamour
When they said goodbye to Greg The Hammer.
Greg was not missed a bit
'Cause of Corby's sharp wit
And he also improved Hardline's grammar.

BEN AND SKIN

Every Friday around 5:20pm, Ben and Skin tolerate me for ten minutes on The Fan.

On Fridays with Ben and with Skin,
Some news of the Rangers I spin.
Sometimes it's a chore,
To not be a bore,
And say things that cause you to grin.

And maybe I'll show you new tunes,
And not just some guy playing spoons.
Great bands at Granada,
The Kessler and Dada,
Many more, if this season's in ruins.

THE FAN

Gavin Spittle is the Program Director at 105.3 The Fan and makes all the high-stakes programming decisions.

Sometimes I'm on with G-Bag Nation,
Who sometimes deserve an ovation,
Or with Corey and Kevin,
Whose show runs til eleven.
Guess night owls are tuned to the station.

At daybreak: Shariff and RJ,
With whom many folks start their day.
Far too early for me
To join Shan and Choppy
Unless they slip me extra pay!

Our boss at The Fan, Gavin Spittle
Makes judgments both giant and little.
Will we get a high rating?
It's like high speed dating
Or trying to answer a riddle.

THE BAT MEN OF WARSTIC

*Jack White and Ian Kinsler have teamed up with Ben Jenkins
to create the coolest baseball bats I've ever seen.
Their showroom is in Dallas in Deep Ellum.*

The beautiful bats built by Warstic

Are those big league studs more and more pick.

Made by Jack White and Ian,

Based on what I am seein',

Those guys better make many more quick.

Yes, Jack White - whose records are gold.

And Kinsler, who's still not that old.

While Jack's playing his axe,

Ian's taking his hacks,

As all of these Warstics are sold.

PINCH HITTERS

HICCUPS?

by Ted Nichols-Payne

For the first time in my 40 years in the booth, on June 25, I was overcome by hiccups while on the air. Our engineer wrote this...

As the baseball team started to play,

The announcer was in a bad way.

He would stop and he'd start

But by far the worst part

Was his hiccups would not go away!

My response:

I really did not want to hiccup.

I know it won't help pick a chick up.

You sent every remedy.

You're all far ahead of me.

I felt I was caught in a stickup!

CHOO'S ON FIRST

by Michael Buchanan

Shin Soo-Choo's 52-game on base streak brightened up an otherwise dismal season.

Team performance appears to be cursed.

This year's pain can be lightened by verse.

If Abbot and Costello

Could salute one fine fellow,

They would no doubt say, "Choo is on first."

LECLERC WON'T SCARE

by Michael Buchanan

Michael Buchanan was taken with Rangers reliever Jose Leclerc.

Leclerc is a kid who won't scare.

He retires star hitters with flair.

When teams try to score

With runners galore,

José just replies "au contraire!"

EASY TO CHEW

by James Drago, age 9

To Eric, I want to thank you

For baseball tix and meeting Choo.

We ate lobster and crab

(All of it was real fab).

Boston was fun & easy to chew!

LECLERC TIME

by Fran Farrelly

And now that our closer's Jose,

In the ninth, "It's Leclerc time" they say.

The pressure is real.

It takes nerves of steel

To get three outs and put them away.

GALLO AND THE POPCORN MAN

by Fran Farrelly

Our Gallo is hitting it hard.
So hard it keeps leaving the yard.
Where it lands, he's not choosy,
But it's always a doozy.
The popcorn man must stay on guard.

ROUGNED AND GALLO

by Alice Wood

Observe our men, Rougned and Gallo.
They're young, but then neither one's callow.
When they step to the plate,
whether early or late,
The outfield had best not play shallow.

BELTRE BEGGING TO PLAY

by James Harman

There once was a God called Beltre,
His mitt so hungry that all day,
It would eat flies that popped,
And can-o'-corns, undropped,
But still begging for the next play.

His lumber was red hot, they say,
At bat, smoking meatballs away.
But what cannot be topped,
Is he could not be stopped,
From begging at each game to play.

RULE 5 STEAL

by John E. Hampton

Delino plays center so great.
He's a Rule 5 steal, no debate.
Also, he's aces
When running the bases.
It's sad that he broke his hamate.

KEMP'S MISSION

by Evan Grant

On June 12 at Dodger Stadium, Matt Kemp crashed into Rangers catcher Robinson Chirinos while trying to score. After a brief altercation, both players were ejected.

In the third, Matt Kemp was on a mission.
With Robbie, there was a collision.
Although benches cleared,
Not as bad as we feared,
And umps told them both to go fishin'.

117

WISDOM TO WIN

by Levi Weaver

The first three times Yovani Gallardo pitched for the Rangers, Texas scored at least 10 runs and won the game.

With Cole Hamels likely departing,
Some "wisdom to win" needs imparting.
My first thought: keep scoring
Until it gets boring
Each time that Gallardo is starting.

WALK DAVIS!

by Vivian Casper

Ranger killer Khris Davis had game-winning home runs against the Rangers on consecutive days in late July. Maybe he should be walked intentionally?

Why did Banny not walk Mister Davis,
Whose at-bats were a warning he gave us?
To lose twice to this guy
Is a number too high.
This decision was no way to save us.

DON'T SOUND THE ALARM

by Bruce Davidson

Some fans want to sound the alarm.
But we'll stand on the mound and rearm,
With youngsters and aces,
That the public embraces,
Cuz you can't keep 'em down on the farm

SPIN AND STICKUM

by Levi Weaver

On the subject of spin, there's a thought
That it can't be increased or taught
With mechanics or power
(Or at least so says Bauer)
But stickum will help quite a lot.

A FAN'S LAMENT

by Bob Hough

Netfali came in from the pen,
One strike from a World Series win.
But that damned David Freese
Brought us down to our knees
And we never got that close again.

VIN SCULLY

by Dan Bern

Vin Scully was the voice of the Dodgers when they moved from Brooklyn to LA in 1958, and worked until 2016.

When O'Malley bought Chavez Ravine,

The announcer went west with the team.

A lifetime in the league,

From Jackie to Puig,

But Vin is The Star it would seem.

THE O'S ON 33RD

by Matt Hicks

My broadcast partner Matt Hicks on returning to Baltimore where he watched the Orioles in their heyday.

I watched the O's on 33rd –
Earl's teams were fun, so was "The Bird."
But in twenty-eighteen,
The cupboard is quite lean,
And their won/loss record is absurd.

MISSING GOLD AND BROWN

by Jason Earll

The Padres now wear gray and blue on the road. James Earll misses their old unis.

The Padres have come to town.
Their uniforms make me frown.
The blue is so boring,
The gray leaves me snoring,
Man, do I miss gold and brown!

WINS AND WAISTLINES

by Norm Hitzges

Bartolo Colon inspired more limericks this year than any other player.

Big Sexy's the name for Colon.
Among Latin arms, he stands alone.
He's pitched 21 years
Without drinking Lite beers.
His win total and waistline have grown.

BIG SEXY BIG HEART

by Vivian Casper

It's Big Sexy on hand for the start.
In his part, he'll reveal a big heart.
He will go for a win
'Gainst a team once his "kin"
And in doing so, show off his art.

BIG SEXY AND THE BIBLE

by Dale Hart

Big Sexy was told how to keep
Big hitters from taking it deep.
True pitchers are liable,
It's explained in the Bible.
It says, "What you throw you will reap."

RIDING WITH BARTOLO

by Matt Hicks

*My broadcast partner Matt Hicks wrote of his ride to the
ballpark in Anaheim with Carlos Tocci and Bartolo Colon.*

I rode with Tocci and Colon.

It's better than traveling alone.

One's back in the fold,

The other's quite old.

Of course, we were all on our phone!

JULY SPECULATION

by Jared Sandler

July is full of speculation about upcoming trades. My broadcast partner Jared Sandler described it this way.

July's the month when GM's scheme

Of trades to help realize the dream.

Deadline's approaching,,,

Wonder who's poaching?

'Cause some will soon join a new team.

KEEP BELTRE!

by Mark Oristano

As the trade deadline approached, some fans expressed their desires in limerick form.

A team fundamentally sound

Can never afford to lose ground.

So trades are oft made,

To try and upgrade,

But please, God, keep Beltre around.

ADRIAN, PLEASE!

by Sally Dieb

Sally Dieb is one of many fans expressing the desire for Adrian Beltre to return.

My head says, "Now, Beltre, you do

What's best for your family and you."

But my heart's on its knees

Begging "Adrian, please,

Play one more year, or maybe two."

HAMELS TO THE CUBS

by David Indorf

On July 26, Cole Hamels was traded to the Cubs after rumors he would be going back to the Phillies.

The thought was he'd go to the Phils

Hoping he'd cure all their ills.

But the Cubbies were clear,

"Hey come over here!

We want you atop Wrigley's hill."

KEEP KELA

by William in Brisbane, Australia

So Colbert is now on the move.
So now will this team find their groove?
Please don't trade Kela.
His career will be stellar
And all we can do is improve.

HARRY AND MEGHAN

by Matt Hicks

Prince Harry and Meghan tied the knot.
Windsor Castle on the Thames was the spot.
Weddings this historic
Give rise to euphoric
Expressions that won't soon be forgot.

NADEL-HICKS TRADE RUMORS

by Levi Weaver

A source says that Hicks and Nadel
Have drawn some trade interest, as well.
Said Dipoto to Daniels,
"Them, plus Weaver and Hamels
And my, how our press box would gel."

ERIC'S RHYME

by Colin Willis

So Eric's been touched by the rhyme,
And his rhyming is simply divine.
He has meter and pace
And good structure in place,
Likely helped by tequila and lime.

WORDSMITHING TRICKS

by Michael Buchanan

Our radio announcer Nadel
Composed lim'ricks that all thought quite swell.
With his partner Matt Hicks,
He used wordsmithing tricks
To pass time when game's hard to sell.

NADEL A POET?

by David Bauer

Many of my friends were taken aback by my new limerick skills.

How does my friend named Nadel

Do all things exceedingly well?

He can spot a great song,

Call home runs all night long.

He's a poet now? Oh what the hell!

NOT A LIMERICK FAN

by Kelly Copeland

And in the 'you can't please everyone' department...

I'm not a big limerick fan.
I'll ignore them whenever I can.
But, I love the Rangers
So, I'll be no stranger.
And you're still the best radio man!

NADEL TRAPPED IN HELL

by Ken Levine

Emmy Award-winning comedy writer Ken Levine provided this one.

Announcer Eric Nadel
Trapped in six months of hell
Started writing for fun,
Cause his team never won,
And now he has a book to sell.

NATIONAL LIMERICK DAY

by Carol Girvin

May 12th – National Limerick Day
Was the day when I entered the fray.
Sandler, Hicks and Nadel
Over me cast a spell;
With limericks I just HAD to play!

It seemed oh so simple, at start,
To make a small verse from my heart.
I became aware
That words do not pair
So easy, till I do my part.

Since lines must often be shuffled;
With many words I must struggle
To fit into my rhyme
With my rhythm and time,
To sooth my mental kerfuffle.

A TRICKY ENDEAVAH

by Levi Weaver

*I challenged my sportswriting friends to write a
limerick about Isiah Kiner-Falefa. Levi Weaver of
The Athletic came up with the best one.*

A limerick's a tricky endeavah.

Puts on some additional pressure.

I will need some more time,

'Cause nothing else will rhyme,

With Isiah Kiner-Falefa!

A MAN WITHOUT EQUALS

by Matt Hicks

*My broadcast partner Matt Hicks put into words
our feelings about the amazing Mike Trout.*

Here's a man without equals, Mike Trout.

This guy's defense is stellar, no doubt.

Whether back to the wall

Or coming in on a ball

He's superb.... plus, we can't get him out.

LEARN, DAN BERN

by Eric Nadel and Dan Navarro

Dan Bern is an enormously talented singer-songwriter who lost the tips of two fingers in a snow blower accident last January. Fortunately, he was back playing guitar by the end of the summer. I wrote this limerick as a tribute to Dan and another wonderful singer-songwriter Dan Navarro added his tribute.

The always amusing Dan Bern
Did something from which he should learn.
When it comes to snow blowing,
Or even yard mowing,
He should let someone else take his turn.

Without even playing guitar,
He's gifted enough to go far.
But I tell you this Bern
Is as nuts as Bruce Dern,
So please keep him out of the bar!

We're glad he's back strumming his song,
Delighting from here to Hong Kong.
His verses are rhymin'
(Not quite like Paul Simon)
We hope nothing else will go wrong.

Dan Navarro chipped in with this:
Now Dan is a really great singer,
With pow'r in his words that can linger.
In truth or in jest
He'll give you his best.
Just don't let him give you the finger!

This limerick thing's been a mystery,

A gift, kind of like a sweet kiss for me.

Thanks for tolerating,

For praise and berating,

And with that I say, "This book is history!"

ABOUT *the* AUTHOR

Eric Nadel just completed his 40th year broadcasting Texas Rangers baseball games on the Texas Rangers Radio Network. The 2014 winner of the Ford C. Frick Award from the National Baseball Hall of Fame, Nadel has also broadcast minor league hockey and women's basketball.

An avid music fan, Nadel promotes several charity concerts each year and is constantly seeking new musical finds and words that rhyme with Kiner-Falefa and Bibens-Dirkx.

He has served as a spokesman and advocate for Focus on Teens, Café Momentum, Campaign to Change Direction and Okay to Say, and the Texas Rangers Baseball Foundation. He also supports various animal rescue organizations.

Nadel previously published three books, "The Man Who Stole First Base… Tales from Baseball's Past," with Craig R. Wright, "The Night Wilt Scored 100… Tales from Basketball's Past," and "Texas Rangers, The Authorized History."

He lives in Dallas, Texas and Durango, Colorado, with his wife Jeannie and dog Kirby, a terrier mix named after Kirby Puckett.

(ISBN: 9781732892705)

Made in the USA
San Bernardino, CA
23 May 2020